Movement Activities for Children with Learning Difficulties

Bren Pointer

Jessica Kingsley Publishers
London and Philadelphia

First published in the United Kingdom in 1993 by
Jessica Kingsley Publishers Ltd
116 Pentonville Road
London N1 9JB

371.92 Poi

57696

Copyright © 1993 Bren Pointer

British Library Cataloguing in Publication Data

Pointer, Bren
Movement Activities for Children with
Learning Difficulties
I. Title
371.92

A10087

ISBN 1 85302 167 9

Printed and Bound in Great Britain by
Cromwell Press, Melksham, Wiltshire

Contents

This book is dedicated to Mary, Jack and Martha,
for all the love, laughter and late nights.

Acknowledgements

My warmest thanks go to the following people without whose help and inspiration this book would not be possible:

The adults at The Causeway Social Education Centre, New Malden.

The staff and children at Hay Lane School and Our Lady of Grace Junior School, London Borough of Brent.

Muke Sullivan and Joe Santamaria, Physical Education and Political Consultants.

Mr Glen Jones, the motivator.

Roger, Arthur, Angus and all at UK Sports Association

Marguerite and Hugh, high order pedagogues of life and love

Sinclair Lewis, Bill Frisell, Jan Garbarek and Robbie Pointer for their insights and celebrations.

Margaret Sleeman, Advisor of PE and Dance, London Borough of Brent

Hyams, Higgins and Praill, from The Coles Green Academy

Carole Duell, for her typing and advice

Mary Mackenzie, my partner in crime.

'Physical Education is concerned with providing experiences that will enable youngsters to become literate in movement to a degree that is relevant, appropriate and applicable to their individual potential.'

Bren Pointer

Introduction

This book offers a variety of movement ideas in the form of
activities for teachers and others involved in educating children
with learning difficulties.

The activities are designed in such a way that they can be
adapted or modified to cater for a wide range of abilities. Children
with learning difficulties do not form a homogeneous group. They
are all different and have different needs. Providing quality movement activities and experiences for children with learning difficulties can be a demanding task and will require the appreciation
of a range of factors which characterize both the way children
learn in movement and how learning can serve to enhance and
encourage quality of life.

Part of a teacher's responsibility is to cater for individual needs
which will entail careful consideration and thought given to the
planning, preparation and organisation of every lesson. This will
help to explain why the book is divided into four sections:

1. Warm up activities

2. Pair activities

3. Small group activities

4. Large group activities

Structured in this way, teachers may find it easier to select
different activities from different sections in order to give balance

and continuity to their lesson organisation. The value of each activity within the book will depend not only upon what is taught but upon how it is taught. This will require great observation and sensitivity on the part of the teacher in terms of assessing the suitability and relevance of an activity in meeting an individual need.

Each activity carries a movement objective or 'activity value' which will, I hope help to inform teachers as to the compatibility of the activity to a specific movement need. The various games may also be useful in embroidering already existing schemes of work in operation in schools at either a basic familiarization level or in more advanced areas.

The National Curriculum Physical Education proposals recommend a balanced PE programme underpinned by four principles to include children with special educational needs:

- Entitlement
- Accessibility
- Integration
- Integrity

It is hoped that the activities contained within this book will help to promote these principles and serve to generate further investigation into physical activity.

The principle of integration for children with learning difficulties into mainstream schools, especially in physical education, will require a commitment from all teachers in order to cope successfully and safely with the challenging demands that such opportunities will present. Teachers, in both special and mainstream schools, will have to familiarize themselves with the possible reasons and causes that lie behind why some children find the physical education experience both difficult and threatening – and ultimately unsuccessful – and the vital cues to look for in identifying such children within a mixed ability population.

Identifying needs within physical education can be a complex and demanding task as there may be considerable needs to identify. A child displaying a learning difficulty may have no obvious physical disability, which will make the question of identification much harder. Children of different ages and stages of development have different needs, children of different aptitudes and abilities have different needs and children with different interests, attitudes and concentration spans all have different needs. Realistically, teachers must decide for themselves what needs they are catering for, which in physical education may not necessarily be solitary physical or motor ones but also embrace social, emotional and cognitive growth. There are, however, various characteristics which may indicate possible learning difficulties among individual children, remembering, as Horvat (1990) explains, that a child might exhibit one or more of them at various levels of severity.

1. **Hyperactivity** – aimless, constant motion around the room or rocking back and forth.

2. **Perceptual-motor impairments** – inability to perceive or interpret sensory stimuli.

3. **Emotional activity** – low frustration tolerance and/or poor self-concept.

4. **General gross motor deficits** – generally unco-ordinated in relation to gross motor skills.

5. **Disorders of attention** – inability to focus on a task, switch tasks or stay with a particular part of a task.

6. **Impulsivity** – inappropriate sudden reaction to a variety of stimuli.

7. **Disorders of memory** – difficulty with short or long term memory.

8. **Disorders of language** – problems with articulation, expressive or receptive language.

A child might not display any of these characteristics but still have difficulties in learning or motor performance in physical education. Murdoch (1985) proposes that either the child's difficulties lie in an inability to use the information given and produce an adequate response or that a child's failure to cope is attributed to a curriculum not suited to the child's needs.

A child's inability to use information and produce adequate responses may be caused by a delay or deprivation in early motor development which will create obvious difficulties in locomotion and co-ordination as well as vital sensorial and motor experiences. In order to achieve effective growth and development, the child progresses through a definite series of movements and activities within given periods of time, laying the foundation for much of its later learning. As the British Association of Advisers and Lecturers in Physical Education (B.A.A.L.P.E. (1989)) explains, the normal sequence of events in motor development tends to follow a pattern:

- reflexive movements (non voluntary) give way to voluntary movements, i.e., movements controlled by the child;

- control is gained first of the head and gradually moves down to the toes (top to bottom);

- muscular control starts by being more effective in the middle of the body before moving outwards to the extremities;

- the clusters of muscles known as the gross motor muscles, controlling movements such as bending over and running, begin to function efficiently before the fine motor muscles, which control more precise and variable actions, for instance the fingers picking up a small object, the use of the mouth in speech, eye movement etc.

A child with learning difficulties may have missed out or been deprived of certain stages of development fundamental to its motor function. Retracing essential movement patterns may give the child the opportunity to fulfil its movement potential in a way that may have otherwise been denied. It is crucial, therefore, that teachers have a basic knowledge of the patterns of normal growth and understand what is meant by good early movement experience.

Teachers will also need to be aware of placing movement activities within a progressive and carefully structured learning environment and understand the mechanisms of how children learn, be able to identify the breakdown of ineffectual and inefficient motor function, and successfully operate a programme of intervention with the child very much as the focus. Taking this into account, the enthusiasm of the teacher in shaping the general atmosphere and sense of enjoyment in the lessons will be essential to its overall success. The range of considerations that teachers need to be aware of will include such factors as time allocation, facilities, number of staff available but, probably most important, knowing the child. However, included below is a summary of teaching guidelines and strategies that will enhance the movement experiences presented to a child with learning difficulties.

Adapting equipment

1. Choose equipment that is bright and colourful wherever possible.

2. Try to provide equipment that is adaptive to ensure success for children, e.g. large sponge balls for hockey.

3. Be flexible and imaginative with equipment (balloons can be relevant learning tools, as they move slowly through the air and are easy to follow).

4. Be prepared to vary the size, texture, weight, length or height of equipment, so that success is achieved.

5. Keep rules simple and modify them if needed so that they are understood by all the children.

Teaching or learning experiences

1. Teachers must be prepared to modify their teaching styles or approaches to accommodate a wide variety of needs.

2. Treat each child as an individual, and remember, what might work with one child may not necessarily work with another.

3. Try to plan activities which provide initial success and will foster confidence, generate further enquiry and give children a sense of achievement.

4. Teachers must keep tasks simple, which will involve using plain understandable language and communicating simply, effectively and economically.

5. Teachers may have to modify the task or break down a skill in order to make learning easier for the children. They will need to be aware of the phases of motor development and identify the stage a child is at within that development.

6. It is important that teachers give positive feedback and praise to the children, so that they can appreciate and gauge the quality of their movement responses.

General

1. If appropriate, use movement education as a medium for learning in other areas. Communication, socialization, numeracy and literacy skills etc, can all be developed through movement. *Think* about individual needs for the whole child, not just the physical domain.

2. Be flexible and imaginative in lessons and, by observation, modify the content accordingly.

3. Try to ensure a progressive and structured learning programme for the children. Lessons should show continuity from week to week, and also offer a balance where the aims are specific but the diet varied.

4. If possible, involve the children in more decision making opportunities at the planning, performing and evaluation stages.

5. Record, monitor and assess the progress of *all* your children on a regular basis.

6. Try to ensure that you have clear intentions as to what you want to achieve in each lesson and over a programme of work.

7. The lessons themselves should involve the children actively and aim to be satisfying, worthwhile and enjoyable experiences for all.

The scenario for physical education provision is changing to give children more decision making opportunities in the planning, performing and evaluation stages of their learning. These developments should not be denied to pupils with learning difficulties but should be reflected in the design and construction of schemes of work and lesson plans within schools catering for a wide variety of extreme learning needs. If, in any way, this book will help towards kick starting the process in creating quality physical education opportunities for children with learning difficulties, it will have served its purpose.

References

B.A.A.L.P.E. (1989) *Physical Education for Children with Special Educational Needs in Mainstream Education*. Leeds: White Line Press.

Horvat, M. (1990) *Physical Education and Sport for Exceptional Students*. Dubuque, Iowa: William C. Brown Publishers.

Murdoch, E. (1985) 'Children with Motor Learning Difficulties.' Paper presented on DES short course: *'Physical Education for Pupils and Students with Special Educational Needs'*. Durham University.

1 Warm Up Activities

The warm up is an essential prerequisite to any form of progressive physical activity. It is crucial to the development and preparation of such areas as muscle toning, cardio-vascular improvement and a general physical preliminary in readiness for further movement demands and challenges. As a body tuning up period, the warm up may, for example, include a variety of stretches to reduce muscle tension, increase flexibility and make the body more relaxed.

However, the activities contained in this section are of more of an active nature and can be used to promote and enhance such areas as social interaction, communication and co–operation, as well as the major physical objectives associated with warm up practices.

For children with learning difficulties, the warm up is especially important in generating an atmosphere conducive to learning and in creating an enjoyable and stimulating framework upon which other movement experiences can take place.

Movement introduction

ACTIVITY — All the children stand in a large circle. One at a time they have to introduce themselves with a movement of any kind. This can be from the most flamboyant to a slight shrug of a shoulder. Everyone in the circle repeats the movement once and then the next person has a turn. This continues until everyone has introduced themselves.

ACTIVITY VALUE — Social development and imaginative way of communicating through movement.

NB Teachers must use good observational skills to include movements or reactions however minimal they appear to be.

Confined space

ACTIVITY — The group walk around the hall freely without touching anyone. They walk forwards, backwards, sideways etc., and explore different directions. This is repeated with only half the hall being used, then only a quarter, until all the class are confined to a relatively small space which can be marked out by either cones or chalk. They have to try and control their speed, balance and co-ordination by avoiding contact with others in a very small area.

NB Not too small to be of danger.

VARIATION
- Use a variety of travelling actions which must be performed in an open then a confined space.

ACTIVITY VALUE — Spatial awareness.

Group numbers

ACTIVITY　　　　The children jog lightly anywhere around the hall. The teacher then calls out a number and the children huddle together in groups of that number as quickly as they can. The game is repeated with a different number being called every time.

VARIATIONS
- Select a child to call the numbers out.
- Keep the children active by varying the movements (crawling on all fours, sliding on backs etc.)

ACTIVITY
VALUE　　　　　Social interaction, spatial awareness and formulating number concepts.

Touch a colour

ACTIVITY　　　　The children jog around the hall. The teacher shouts out a colour and the children run and touch that colour, which may be around the hall or on a child's clothing.

ACTIVITY
VALUE　　　　　Social interaction, spatial awareness and recognising colour.

Clap hands, stamp feet

ACTIVITY

The children form a large circle and clap their hands very lightly, gradually getting faster and louder. They then repeat this using their feet, tapping lightly and gradually stamping quickly and loudly. Finally, they all sit down with their hands by their sides, bend their knees and tap their feet lightly and then firmly and as fast as they can.

VARIATION

- Can the children clap hands and stamp feet at the same time?
- Can the children wave with their hands and feet?

ACTIVITY VALUE

Group co-operation and co-ordinating different body parts.

Body parts in hoop

ACTIVITY

Hoops are spread around the hall. The children run around the hoops without touching each other. The teacher calls out a part of the body and the children must place that body part inside the hoop. The activity continues until a variety of body parts have been called.

VARIATIONS

- When a body part is called out, the children have to make sure it is the highest body part in the air.
- The children can be chosen to call out a body part.

EQUIPMENT

Hoops.

ACTIVITY VALUE

Recognition of different body parts, spatial awareness and developing reaction time.

Walls

ACTIVITY The walls in the hall are numbered 1, 2 and 3. The children line up along wall number 1 and are given a variety of instructions, for example, 'crawl to wall number 3', 'hop to wall number 2', 'slide on backs to wall number 3' etc. Try to catch the children out by saying 'sprint to wall number 5'.

VARIATIONS
- Use colours instead of numbers.
- Vary the tasks, e.g. only children with black hair to wall number 2, children with blue eyes to wall number 1 etc.

ACTIVITY VALUE Co-ordinating activity task with direction, which involves relating comprehension of task and memory.

Get in order

ACTIVITY
1. *Of height* – The children line up against the wall. On the teacher's instruction, they organize themselves into a line with the smallest child at one end and ending with the tallest at the other.
2. *Alphabetical order* – As above but instead of height first names are used: the line begins with 'A' one end and progresses to 'Z' at the other.

VARIATIONS
- In order of birthdays with the line running from January until December.
- In order of hair colour, starting with fair hair and progressing to black or dark hair.

ACTIVITY VALUE Co-operation, social interaction, visual judgement and discrimination.

Here, there, everywhere

ACTIVITY

The children move around the hall as directed by the teacher and listen for the teacher to call out either 'Here', 'There' or 'Everywhere'. 'Here' means that, wherever the teacher is situated in the hall the children have to run to him or her. 'There' means the children have to run to wherever the teacher is pointing and 'Everywhere' means that the teacher is trying to tag the children so they must run everywhere to avoid being tagged.

ACTIVITY VALUE

Perceptual awareness, spatial awareness, developing reaction time and physical response to commands.

Hand shake

ACTIVITY

The children walk around the hall shaking hands with each other and introducing themselves to one another. They then repeat this but jog round slowly and shake hands.

ACTIVITY VALUE

Social interaction and co-operation.

Back to back

ACTIVITY

The children move around the hall to music as specified by the teacher. When the music stops, they have to get back to back with someone as quickly as possible until the music starts again. Every time the music stops they have to find a different partner to go back to back with.

ACTIVITY
VALUE

Develops audio–visual co-ordination and social interaction through physical contact.

Pick up

ACTIVITY

The class is divided into two groups. The teacher has a bucket of red and yellow balls which are thrown around the hall. One team has to collect all the yellow balls and the other all the red balls as quickly as they can and deposit them in trays or boxes at opposite ends of the hall.

VARIATION

- More teams can be used provided more coloured balls are available.

EQUIPMENT

Lots of balls of two different colours.

ACTIVITY
VALUE

Spatial awareness, fine motor co-ordination and eye–hand co-ordination.

Body point

ACTIVITY	The children form a semi-circle around the teacher either sitting down or standing up. The teacher calls out parts of the body and, as quickly as they can, the children must touch that body part.
VARIATIONS	• The children stand in a semi-circle but must rub or 'wash' different body parts as directed by the teacher, for example washing hair and progressing down the body to rub the toes! • A child could choose the body parts to be touched.
ACTIVITY VALUE	Recognising and knowing where different body parts are.

Circle exercises

ACTIVITY	The children hold hands in a circle. The teacher then calls out a variety of tasks that the children have to perform all together and still holding hands. For example, kneel down, hop on the spot, two footed jump on the spot, sit down.
VARIATIONS	• Divide the group into smaller circles if there are too many children. • Begin the activity and tasks slowly so that the children can grasp the demands successfully.
ACTIVITY VALUE	Physical fitness, co-operation and social development.

Back to back tag

ACTIVITY   The group is divided into pairs of relatively the same height and weight. Each pair goes back to back and links arms. One pair are chosen to be the 'taggers' and stand at one end of the hall. They could wear bibs to identify themselves. On the word 'go' they move round the hall trying to touch other pairs who, if tagged, must put on bibs and join in the tagging. This continues until all the pairs are caught.

VARIATION   • It may be useful to walk this activity through first until the children can successfully move back to back with their partners.

EQUIPMENT   Bibs or coloured bands.

ACTIVITY   Partnership co-operation and co-ordination.
VALUE

Blue line, red line

ACTIVITY   This activity can be played in a gym or hall where there are floor court markings laid down of various colours and lines. The children move around the hall as described by the teacher, and when the teacher calls out a colour, they must stand on that coloured line as quickly as possible.

VARIATIONS • Children can sit or lie down on the line.

            • The teacher could call 'curved' or 'straight' to describe the line.

ACTIVITY   Formulating colour concepts, spatial awareness and
VALUE   physical reaction.

Stamp to a letter

ACTIVITY

The children are divided into pairs and numbered 1 and 2. All the number 1s run around the hall and try to get away from their partners, number 2s, who try to keep as close as they can to them. When the teacher blows the whistle, everybody stops still so he or she can see the distance between the pairs. They then change over and number 2s have to get away from number 1s.

ACTIVITY VALUE

Spatial and perceptual awareness, physical agility and tracking skills.

Pull the bib

ACTIVITY

A variation of 'stamp to a letter'. In pairs number 1s have a bib or coloured band tucked out from their shorts like a tail. On the teacher's whistle, number 2s have to chase their partner and try to snatch the tail from their partners' shorts. They then change over.

VARIATION

• Only two or three children in the class are without bibs, and they have to chase everyone else and try to snatch as many bibs as they can.

EQUIPMENT

Coloured bibs or bands.

ACTIVITY VALUE

Spatial awareness, physical agility and tracking skills.

Points of contact

ACTIVITY
The children are spaced around the hall and the teacher explains that 'points of contact' means the number of body parts (or contacts) that are touching the floor at any one time. For example, standing still has two points of contact, the left foot and the right foot. The children are then asked to demonstrate a variety of points of contact with the floor which the teacher chooses by calling out a number – children must have that number of body parts touching the floor.

ACTIVITY VALUE
Decision making (which body parts to use), numeracy development and physical agility (especially in challenging positions of stillness).

29

Left or right

ACTIVITY The children form a line one behind the other down the middle of the hall. The teacher calls out either left or right. On the command 'left', the children have to side step to the left wall and back to the middle. This activity must be started slowly so that the children understand their left and right sides.

VARIATION • Colours can be used to help determine left or right sides, e.g. blue for left, red for right.

ACTIVITY VALUE Physical fitness and development of knowledge of left and right.

Freeze!

ACTIVITY The children move around the hall as directed by the teacher. On the command 'freeze' everyone must stand absolutely still. They hold a position of stillness for five seconds and then move round the hall in a different way than before.

ACTIVITY VALUE Listening skills, physical control and development of maintaining a position of stillness.

Open leg tag

ACTIVITY
One child is chosen to be the tagger trying to touch the rest of the class moving round the hall. If touched, the children have to stand still with their arms spread and their legs open. They can be 'released' only by untagged children crawling through their legs. The game continues for either a set time or until all children are tagged.

VARIATION
• More than one tagger begins the game.

ACTIVITY
VALUE
Physical fitness, spatial and perceptual awareness.

Hoops and cones

ACTIVITY
Hoops and cones are spread around the hall. The children move around the hall as directed by the teacher and on the command 'hoop' they must stand in a hoop, 'cone' they must stand by a cone and 'hoops and cones' they must have part of their body in a hoop and another part touching a cone. Ensure that hoops and cones are spread equally around the hall!

EQUIPMENT
Hoops and cones.

ACTIVITY
VALUE
Rapid decision making, physical agility.

Roll-a-hoop

ACTIVITY

The children jog lightly around the hall while the teacher stands behind a line at one end with a hoop. On the teacher's whistle, the children all lie down still. The teacher then rolls the hoop to try and touch someone. If successful, the child who was touched joins the teacher behind the line. The children get up and move round again until the whistle is blown and they then lie down. The hoops are then rolled again and those touched join the group rolling the hoops. This is repeated until all the children are touched by the hoops.

VARIATIONS

- Quoits can be used instead of hoops.
- Children can either stand or sit when the whistle is blown.
- Hoops or quoits can be rolled one at a time.

EQUIPMENT

Enough hoops for one per child.

ACTIVITY VALUE

Eye–hand co-ordination, maintaining stillness and listening skills.

Peg walk

ACTIVITY

Each child is given a few clothes pegs which they attach to any part of their clothing. They then move around the hall trying to shake the pegs off. If they fall off, they attach them to a different part of their clothing.

VARIATION

- In pairs (either standing, sitting or kneeling) the children have to attach themselves to each other with the pegs. They can try and move around the hall without unattaching themselves.

EQUIPMENT

Clothes pegs.

ACTIVITY VALUE

Fine motor skills, eye–hand co-ordination, social co-operation.

The cassette game

The teacher tells the children that they are all cassettes inside a cassette recorder and have to respond with certain movements to some 'cassette tasks' that the teacher calls out. For example:

- PLAY means walking around the hall
- FAST FORWARD means jogging around the hall
- REWIND means walking backwards
- EJECT means star jumping on the spot
- RECORD means spinning on tummies lying on the floor
- STOP means stop!

The tasks are introduced gradually so the children grasp the word with its corresponding action. The children can make up their own actions to more cassette type instructions.

VARIATIONS This type of word association activity can also be explored in other subject areas. For example, various beans can be used in a similar way:

- 'Frozen beans' means freeze
- 'Jumping beans' means jump
- 'Runner beans' means jog around
- 'Chilli beans' means running on the spot rubbing with arms to keep warm
- 'Baked beans' means lying on backs in a star shape.

Other actions can be added depending on the type of bean, of course!

ACTIVITY VALUE Responding and reacting to tasks, using memory, physical fitness and a great deal of fun.

2 Pair Activities

Working with a partner can provide a host of advantageous possibilities. Children can learn not only a variety of motor skills and an increased movement vocabulary, but acquire essential skills in building relationships with each other and understanding and appreciating body management and control. Veronica Sherborne (1990), the pioneering movement specialist, suggested that partner activities can be classified under three headings:

1. Caring or 'with' activities, which include partnerships in which one partner both contains and supports another.

2. Shared relationships, where partners learn how to support each other and at the same time how to trust each other with their weight.

3. 'Against' relationships, where partners test each other's strength and stability.

The activities in this section include examples of these principles but also practices which promote gross and fine motor skills and co-ordination. These acquired skills may form the basis or the keys which lead into an increased movement repertoire and competence, which may give youngsters with learning difficulties opportunities for participation in a much wider field of activity.

However, this may well depend on individual capabilities, what type of skill is being learnt and the relevance of the learning experience to the individual's movement potential.

I hope these examples may be effective in their own right, but also used as a vehicle through which other learning possibilities might be examined.

Tandem cycling

ACTIVITY

A and B lie down on the floor opposite each other so that the soles of their feet are touching. They then lift their legs up off the floor and start to cycle against each other. This is best achieved doing it slowly at first and gradually speeding up until a steady rhythmic motion is maintained.

ACTIVITY
VALUE

Co-operation, timing and motor co-ordination.

Hoop bridge

ACTIVITY

Partner A makes a bridge shape on the floor ensuring that either his or her legs or hands are placed inside a hoop. Partner B then has to guide the hoop from the hands back to the feet or the feet up to the hands, without touching their partner's body. This is similar to guiding an electric loop through a wire at funfairs. If it touches the wire a bell rings. The hoop must be guided slowly up or down the body. Explore different bridge shapes and change over.

EQUIPMENT

One hoop per pair.

ACTIVITY
VALUE

Maintaining balance and stillness, eye–hand co-ordination, controlling and guiding skills.

Bench pass

ACTIVITY — A and B sit facing each other on a bench, a small distance apart. They push a sponge ball towards each other so that it rolls along the bench without falling off. As they become competent, they can widen the distance between them.

VARIATIONS

- They have to roll the ball to each other for a set time counting the number of passes made.

- Individually, they stand by the side of the bench, put the ball on it and, using fingers only, roll the ball down the bench while walking. This can be repeated and speeded up.

- If the bench is heightened at one end, a child can place the ball at the high end, let it go and try to catch it when it drops off at the other end.

EQUIPMENT — Benches and balls.

ACTIVITY VALUE — Eye–hand co-ordination, aiming, sending and receiving skills and fine motor co-ordination.

Cradling

ACTIVITY

Partner A sits behind partner B and straddles or cradles them with legs astride. They squash up tight against each other and slowly, by Shuffling on their bottoms and pushing into the floor with their hands, move forward around the hall in this cradled position.

VARIATIONS

- Explore alternative ways of moving in this position (forwards, backwards, sideways etc.)
- Two pairs or more can join up to create a longer line, almost caterpillar like, of cradled children moving slowly around the hall.

ACTIVITY
VALUE

Co-operation and trust.

High jump

ACTIVITY

Partner A faces a wall in the hall, does a standing jump and touches the wall at the highest point of the jump with his or her hand. Partner B, who is standing on a chair or a bench next to partner A, marks with chalk the point of contact made from partner A's hand with the wall. The distance between the chalk mark and the height of the jumper is measured and recorded and the partners swap over.

VARIATION

- This can be also employed in a long jump exercise where the distance jumped is measured by a chalk mark.

EQUIPMENT

Chalk and chair per pair.

ACTIVITY VALUE

Development of basic movement action (jumping), and placing responsibility of recording, measuring and evaluating jump in the hands of the children themselves.

Ball passing

ACTIVITY

The children are divided into pairs and stand back to back against each other. Each pair has one ball. Player A holds the ball in two hands and turns to the side, without moving his or her feet, and hands the ball to player B who has also turned to the side to collect the ball. Player B then turns and brings the ball to the other side where player A has also turned to collect it. This process of collecting and turning is repeated.

VARIATIONS

- Instead of passing the ball from side to side while the pairs are back to back, the ball can also be passed – 'over and under' – over the heads and through the legs whilst still remaining back to back.

- A time limit can be set on how many passes can be made; for example, in one minute or 30 seconds.

EQUIPMENT

One ball per pair.

ACTIVITY VALUE

Developing ball skills in both handling and giving and receiving (releasing and retaining), also eye–hand co-ordination.

See-saw

ACTIVITY

Partner A lies down on his or her back. Partner B lies face down in a press up position on top of A although at opposite ends. Partner A then pushes B's legs up at the time when partner B has lowered A's legs, and when B straightens his or her arms, partner A lowers partner B's legs! This is repeated to get a see-saw effect. The positions of partners can then change over.

ACTIVITY
VALUE

Developing muscular strength (lifting and lowering), co-ordination of alternate movements.

Duck walk

ACTIVITY

Standing back to back the children bend down with their legs open and hold on to each other's left hand through each other's legs. They then begin to walk either forwards, backwards or sideways in this position.

ACTIVITY
VALUE

Co-operation and communication.

Envelopes

ACTIVITY

Partner A gets on hands and knees and partner B slides underneath so that A envelopes or encases his or her partner. They then move slowly round the hall in this way with A on all fours and B sliding on their fronts underneath. They then change over.

ACTIVITY
VALUE

Trust and security and co-operation working with a partner.

Wall walk

ACTIVITY

Working individually or in pairs the children spread out around the hall and lie down on their backs with their feet flat against the hall wall. They must then see how far they can walk up the wall, keeping their hands on the hall floor and pushing upwards. Their partners can chalk up a mark as to how far they go. This activity can also be done by lying on stomachs with feet against the wall and by walking up the wall and pushing up with their hands and arms. See if they can get into a handstand position against the wall.

ACTIVITY
VALUE

Development of strength in arms, taking weight on hands and maintaining body weight support.

NB Ensure this activity is done on mats, one per child.

Back to back stand up

ACTIVITY

In pairs sitting back to back with arms linked, the children must try to stand up by bending their knees and pushing against each other slowly.

ACTIVITY VALUE

Co-operation, leg strength and co-ordination in pairs.

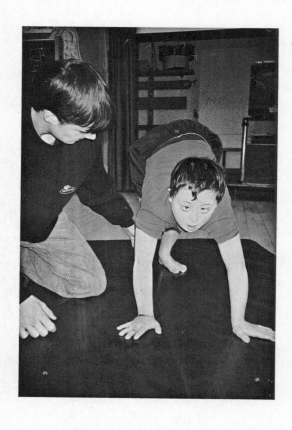

Tunnels and bridges

ACTIVITY   Partner A makes a bridge shape on hands and knees. Arms and knees must be fairly wide open. To make the bridge higher legs can be straightened with bottoms pointing in the air! Partner B must crawl in between the gaps or tunnels that partner A forms. They then change over.

VARIATION
- All partner As in the class are bridges and their partners go through as many tunnels as they can and crawl and slide from one child toanother. Change over.

ACTIVITY VALUE   Basic body movement (crawling), and maintaining a stable base on four body points (hands and knees).

Stuck to the mat

ACTIVITY   A lies on his or her tummy in a star shape, as if stuck like glue to the mat. Partner B must try and turn them over by up-ending them using their hands. They then change over.

ACTIVITY VALUE   Upper arm strength and ability to resist being lifted by distributing whole body weight.

Star shapes

ACTIVITY

Partner A lies down on his or her back in a star shape. Partner B slowly walks around the gaps that the star shape has made. They then change over.

VARIATION

- All the As lie in a star shape and the Bs walk freely around the hall stepping in between the shapes on the floor. They then change over.

ACTIVITY VALUE

Trust and motor co-ordination.

Bean bag pass

ACTIVITY

Both A and B lie down on their backs with their heads in the centre and their bodies forming a straight line. Partner A has a bean bag placed in between his or her feet. Partner A lifts his or her legs up in the air, trying not to drop the bean bag and trying to pass it to partner B who has come to meet it by also lifting his or her feet up. Once the change has occurred, partner B slowly brings the bean bag down and the process is repeated.

EQUIPMENT

One bean bag per pair.

ACTIVITY VALUE

Eye–foot co-ordination and controlling leg movement and strength.

Roll me down

ACTIVITY

On mats, partner A stands astride over partner B, who is lying on his or her back. Partner B has to roll left or right to try and touch one of partner A's legs. Partner B must have his or her hands down by the sides and roll the whole body to one side or other. The pairs change places once a leg is touched.

ACTIVITY VALUE

Developing side to side rolling, side stepping and lateral movement.

Round the mat

ACTIVITY

Partner A and partner B face each other at opposite ends of a mat in a press up position with only their hands on the mat. On command, partner A chases partner B around the mat – both must travel with only their hands on the mat. Once tagged, they change over and partner B chases partner A.

ACTIVITY VALUE

Weight bearing and travelling on hands, co-ordinating peripheral vision with mobility and physical strength.

Parcels

Partner A lies on a mat and ties him or herself up like a package by crossing legs, folding arms and getting into a shape that is impossible for partner B to undo. Partner B tries to unwrap this human parcel by tugging at arms and legs to try and release them or untie them. Partner B then becomes the parcel and the unpacking starts again.

ACTIVITY
VALUE

Trust and co-operation with partner, strength and passive resistance.

Sliding back to back

ACTIVITY

In pairs, the children sit down back to back with their legs out straight. Partner A pushes partner B around the hall by bending his or her legs and pushing into his or her partners back. Partner B slides around the hall for a minute or so and then they change over.

This activity works more effectively on a shiny floor surface.

NB Match the pairs up of roughly equal height and weight.

ACTIVITY
VALUE

Physical strength and stamina using large muscle movements and co-operation.

Jumping jacks

ACTIVITY

Partner A squats down and faces partner B, who is standing up. They lock wrists so that their grip is secure. The child who is squatting bounces three times before springing up to jump as high as he or she can, supported by his or her partner. This is repeated three times before they change over.

ACTIVITY
VALUE

Trust, co-operation, basic body movements (jumping and springing).

Knee push

ACTIVITY

On mats around the hall, partner As kneel on all fours so that their backs are like table tops. They must imagine being glued in that position. Partner Bs kneel up to the side of partner As and, by placing their hands on partner As' side just above the waist, tries to push them over. Partner As try to resist this pressure. They try this several times before changing over.

ACTIVITY
VALUE

Trust and balance, and 'pushing' strength.

Balls, balloons and bubbles

ACTIVITY

Working in pairs, one partner lies on a mat. A series of balls of varying shapes, sizes, colours and textures are rolled up and down the child's body – tennis balls, sponge balls, air flow balls, table tennis balls etc. Balloons can be dropped and bounced on the child and rolled up and down. Finally bubbles are blown and allowed to rest or burst over the child on different parts of the body. They then change over.

VARIATION

• A gentle warm down at the end of a lesson is to have the group lying down and the teacher blowing bubbles all over them.

EQUIPMENT

Variety of balls, balloons of bright colours and pots of bubbles.

ACTIVITY VALUE

This activity may be of more use to youngsters with mobility difficulties so that they can enjoy the feeling of different balls, balloons and bubbles landing on them, and be stimulated by the colours, textures and weights of the various objects. This will also help to promote eye contact between child and object.

Chalk shapes

ACTIVITY

Partner A lies down on a mat in a star shape on his or her back. Partner B, who has a piece of chalk, simply slowly draws round partner A's body so that the child can feel the shape being drawn. They change over with a different shape being used.

VARIATIONS

- Once all the children's shapes have been drawn, the children can see if they can fit 'inside' someone else's body shape!

- In either small groups or one large circle, the children lie down with their heads in the middle. The teacher, with one or two others, draws round the body shapes of the whole group. The finished product should resemble a flower, that is if everyone keeps still!

EQUIPMENT

Chalk and mats per pair.

ACTIVITY VALUE

Especially beneficial to children with severe mobility difficulties so they can feel involved and participate with others. It also develops fine motor co-ordination (drawing) and stillness.

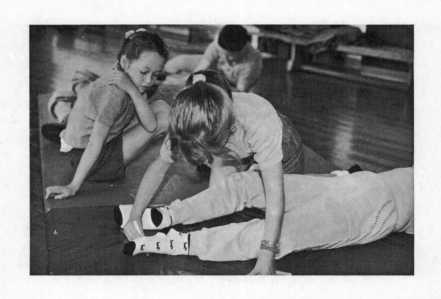

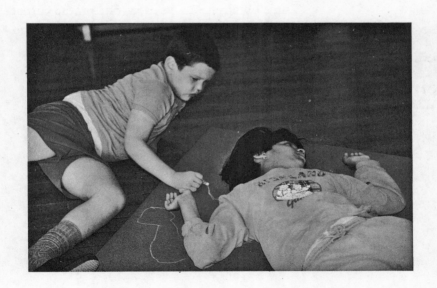

Carpets and hoops

ACTIVITY Partner A has a carpet square and partner B has a hoop. Partner A places the carpet square face down on the floor so that it will slide more easily. He or she then lies on it on his or her chest. Partner B gives A one end of a hoop to hold on to and, while gripping the other end him or herself, proceeds to drag partner A by the hoop around the hall. After a while they change over.

VARIATIONS
- Can partners be dragged in a zigzag line or curvy or straight line?
- Use various obstacles to go through or round to make the slide more exciting and interesting.
- Explore different lying or sitting arrangements on the carpet.
  NB Don't go too fast.
- Three children can be used, one on the carpet and two pulling, explore different combinations.

EQUIPMENT Carpet square and hoop per pair.

ACTIVITY
VALUE Co-operation, physical strength.

Prisoners

ACTIVITY

Partner A sits between the legs of partner B, who then wraps his or her arms and legs around A. Partner A must then try to escape and break loose by pushing away the arms and legs.

NB Children shouldn't wrap themselves too tightly round their partners; just enough to resist passively the pushing and pulling of arms and legs!

ACTIVITY VALUE

Trust, co-operation, strength.

Driver and wheel

ACTIVITY

In pairs facing each other, A puts his or her hands on B's shoulders and has to steer B around the hall by turning the shoulders either left or right without touching any other children. They then change over.

ACTIVITY VALUE

Trust, co-operation and spatial awareness.

Head to head

ACTIVITY   The children are divided into pairs. The teacher then calls out, for example, 'head to head', and the pairs join each other's heads together as quickly as they can. Different body parts are called out to be joined together, for example, shoulder to shoulder or left knee to left knee.

VARIATION   • The teacher calls out two different body parts, e.g. tummy and ear, and the pairs must quickly join them together until the next combination of body parts is called.

ACTIVITY
VALUE   Knowledge of body parts, alertness in reacting quickly to commands and collaborating socially with partner.

Idols

ACTIVITY   Each pair stands one in front of the other, both facing the same way. The child in front (A) puts his or her hands behind his or her back.

Child (B) then puts his or her arms under child A's armpits and in this way becomes A's hands and arms. They now walk around the hall meeting other pairs and shaking hands. After a while they change over.

ACTIVITY
VALUE   Partnership co-operation and co-ordination, social interaction.

Elastic shapes

ACTIVITY

This activity can be played individually, in pairs or in a small group. Each unit has an elastic circle (strips of elastic sewn together at the ends). Individually they can explore its shape-making possibilities by wrapping it round their feet and over their heads etc.

In pairs or small groups, the children can work with the elastic on different levels (one lying, one kneeling, one standing etc.)

VARIATIONS

- Every one in the group must touch the elastic with a different body part, creating exciting and challenging movement positions.

- It may be easier if the teacher demonstrates a movement possibility using the elastic from which the children can progress on their own.

- Remember to use different levels, heights, widths etc to make interesting shapes.

EQUIPMENT   Elastic circles.

ACTIVITY
VALUE   Creative movement, decision making and planning own movement positions, links and sequences.

3 Small Group Activities

The small group games and activities contained in this section offer a variety of experiences and learning opportunities. These range from small sided team games and relays, movement skills and lead-up or progression activities to more complex challenges. Some of the small group practices will be useful in preparation for larger game situations, but the teacher will need to organise the class sensitively so that the transfer of learning from a small to a large environment is successful.

The learning of skills may, for some children, be increasingly beneficial if presented in a conditioned game context and will enhance understanding if the skill is allowed to develop through progressive exposure to various types, albeit related, of game experiences.

Opportunities for children to create their own games, where appropriate, should also be considered. This also provides children with some sense of responsibility for their own learning.

The following activities may help to activate a platform of new ideas and create alternative game learning possibilities.

Spoke wheel relay

ACTIVITY

The teacher draws a large cross with chalk on the hall floor. The children are then divided into four teams. Each team has to sit on a line one behind the other, facing the centre. The first person in each team has a ball which he or she passes overhead to the next person and so on until it reaches the last child at the end of the line. He or she runs clockwise around all the other teams or lines until he/she returns to his/her own and goes to the front of the line, and the sequence is repeated until all the team members have run around the other lines or 'spokes'. The first team to complete their runs are the winners.

VARIATIONS

- Vary the passing of the ball down the line, e.g. side to side, through the legs.
- Vary the method of moving round the hall, e.g. crawling, pigeon steps.
- Benches can be used as the spokes.

EQUIPMENT

Chalk or benches, balls.

ACTIVITY VALUE

Co-operation, fitness, eye–hand co-ordination, spatial awareness.

Grand prix

ACTIVITY

The group is divided into four teams who line up one behind the other at one end of the hall. Every team member has a unihoc stick (a lighter plastic version of a hockey stick) and in front of each team a rubber quoit is placed on the floor. On the word 'go', the first member places the straight end of their hockey stick inside the quoit and, by holding the curved end with his/her hands (rather like a walking stick), drags the quoit along the floor, in and out of cones placed in a line in front of the team. Once round and back, the second person goes, and this continues until all team members have been. The winning team is the first to complete the course.

Guiding the quoit with the hockey stick upside down in this way gives the children great control over it, as it won't run away. A variety of pair activities or individual skill tasks can be presented:

VARIATION

- Push the quoit in and out of legs.
- Push quoit at a target.
- Dribble quoit round various obstacles over a set time.

EQUIPMENT

Unihoc sticks, quoits and cones.

ACTIVITY VALUE

Basic skill learning in propelling and guiding object with unihoc stick, eye–hand co-ordination, spatial awareness and physical fitness.

Bench ball passing

Two teams sit on benches facing each other. The first person at one end of the bench has a ball and on the command 'go' the ball is passed with two hands down the bench until it reaches the last person. On receiving the ball he or she must run round the bench to the front and commence the passing again. Everyone moves or shuffles up to allow the back player enough space at the front. This continues until all team members have run with the ball from the end of the bench to the front.

VARIATIONS

- The ball can be passed down the bench in a variety of ways: side to side, over the head, one handed etc.

- Cones could be used to make the run back with ball more interesting and challenging.

EQUIPMENT

One ball per bench.

ACTIVITY VALUE

Eye–hand co-ordination, basics of passing (giving and receiving), physical fitness.

Crusts or crumbs

ACTIVITY A chalk line is drawn across the middle of the hall. The class is divided into pairs. These pairs sit back to back along this line. The children facing North are the crusts and children facing South are the crumbs. If the teacher calls out 'crusts', the children who are crusts stand up and turn and run to catch the crumbs before they get home. The children who are being chased by the crusts have to run to the end of the hall that they are facing and avoid being tagged. This is reversed if the teachers calls out 'crumbs'. The teacher can hover over the 'cr...' sound, to keep the children in suspense as to whether crusts or crumbs is going to be called out.

ACTIVITY VALUE Developing reaction time and speed in decision making.

Tag the train

ACTIVITY Four or so children form a train by standing in a line and holding each other's waists. The person at the end of the train has a bib or coloured band tucked outside their shorts like a tail. Numerous trains move around the hall trying both to avoid having their tails snatched from them while at the same time the front person tries to steal other trains' tails. This must all be done while the train is fully linked up from child to child!

EQUIPMENT Bibs or coloured bands.

ACTIVITY VALUE Co-operation, perceptual awareness.

Letter shapes

ACTIVITY

This activity can be done in pairs or small groups. A letter of the alphabet is called out by the teacher and the children have to form that letter shape with their bodies. This can be done either standing up, sitting down or lying down. With more children to a group, a word can be made with a variety of different body shapes.

VARIATION

- Let the children decide their own letters for the rest of the class to guess.

ACTIVITY VALUE

Co-operation, imagination and creative movement expression.

Four corner spray

ACTIVITY

Each small group forms a small semi-circle with one child standing in the middle facing the rest of the group. He or she has a ball and passes it to each member, who returns it. When every one has been passed to, the child in the middle returns to the group and the next child comes out and starts the passing again. This continues until every one has had a turn in the middle.

VARIATIONS

- Shorten or lengthen the distance between the central passer, depending on the ability of the group.

- See how many passes can be made in a set time or have a competition with the other groups to see which group completes a circuit of passes first.

- Instead of a semi-circle format, a line can be used whereby a pass is made to each of the children, who are in a line one behind the other, and every time a successful pass is made, they sit down on the floor so that a pass can be made to the child behind them. This continues until all have successfully passed the ball and are all sitting down.

EQUIPMENT

One ball per group.

ACTIVITY VALUE

Catching and passing skills, eye–hand co-ordination.

Rocking and rolling

ACTIVITY   This activity can be done in groups of four. On mats three children get down on their hands and knees in a line, all huddled up, facing the same way. The fourth person simply lies down across the backs of the three children, who then proceed to gently rock forwards and backwards on the spot. They then change the person lying on the top.

NB Use children whose height and weight distribution is similar.

VARIATION
- What other way can the group move? Side to side, in a circular motion, mexican wave undulations?

ACTIVITY VALUE   Co-operation and trust, weight bearing on stable bases and transferring weight distribution.

Hoop balance

ACTIVITY   In threes, the children try to balance a hoop on their heads; they then try and move slowly round the gym keeping the hoop balanced on top. Try and arrange the three children to be of similar height!

VARIATION
- The children can use other body parts to balance the hoop, e.g. shoulders or stomachs.

EQUIPMENT   One hoop per three children.

ACTIVITY VALUE   Co-operation and balance.

Trains to stations

ACTIVITY   In the four corners of the hall the teacher draws large circles with chalk which represent railway stations (for example, Euston, Victoria, Waterloo and Paddington). The children are divided into four teams and each team forms a line holding each other's waists, like a train. On the teacher's instruction, the four trains weave around the hall but when the teacher calls out 'Stations!', each team to make has its way to their respective home stations as quickly as possible, without breaking or letting go waists!

ACTIVITY
VALUE   Working co-operatively as a team.

Tag the tail

ACTIVITY   In groups of four, three children hold hands and form a circle and one child stands outside. One of the three children in the circle has a bib or coloured band hanging outside of their shorts like a tail. The object of the game is for the child outside the circle to try and take the bib from the shorts while the children in the circle try to stop them by moving either clockwise or anti-clockwise, still holding hands. Once stolen, a different child becomes the chaser and a different child becomes the 'tail'.

EQUIPMENT   Bibs or coloured bands.

ACTIVITY
VALUE   Group cohesion and co-operation, visual perception.

Turtle cover

ACTIVITY

Groups of six children huddle on their hands and knees, tightly bunched up, in two rows of three. Their backs should be flat like a table top. A mat is placed on top of them (if the mat is too heavy, a blanket will do). They must then proceed to move to a specified distance, all together, slowly, without dropping the blanket, and maintaining their shape.

EQUIPMENT

Mats or blankets.

ACTIVITY
VALUE

Co-operation and group co-ordination.

Tank tracks

ACTIVITY

Six or so children have two mats. They all stand on one and hold the other above their heads. They must then put the mat down on the ground and all get on it, without touching the floor, and pick up the first mat and repeat the sequence. They continue this way for a specified distance.

EQUIPMENT

Two mats per group.

ACTIVITY
VALUE

Co-operation and team work.

Ankle link

ACTIVITY | Groups of four move around the hall in a line crawling on their hands and knees and holding on to the ankles of the person in front. The group can link up with another group to make eight and crawl like a snake. The whole class could make a large circle and move either forwards or backwards. Please note that knees may get sore, so it is advisable to do this activity on mats or for only a short time on the floor.

ACTIVITY VALUE | Co-operation, synchronized movement.

Pass the hoop

ACTIVITY | The class is divided into groups of five or six children who form a circle and hold hands. A hoop is placed between two children, who hold hands through it, so that it is resting on top of their arms. The children must pass the hoop round the circle by climbing through it, but without letting go of hands.

VARIATIONS

- Instead of only one hoop, two or three hoops are placed around the circle in between children so that less time is spent waiting and more time is spent climbing through hoops.

- Depending on ability, use large or smaller hoops to make the activity either easier or more challenging.

ACTIVITY VALUE | Co-operation and basic body mobility.

Balloon tap

The class is divided into small groups comprising five or six children. They form a circle and hold hands. Each group has a balloon and the object of the game is to keep the balloon up in the air without letting go of hands. Heads, legs, arms etc., can be used to hit the balloon and stop it touching the floor.

VARIATIONS
- The groups have to travel from one end of the hall to the other keeping the balloon up in the air without letting go of hands.
- Count how many taps each group can achieve before the balloon touches the floor.
- The balloon must be passed around the group in sequence.
- Some groups who may find the activity easy can be challenged by only using specific parts of the body, e.g. legs only, heads only etc.

EQUIPMENT Balloons.

ACTIVITY Co-operation, eye–hand/foot co-ordination.
VALUE

Tunnel crawl

The children are organised into groups of three. On their hands and feet they all form bridges in a line, nicely squashed up together. On the word 'go' from the teacher, the child at the end of the line gets down and crawls through the other two bridges and then re-positions him or herself at the front. The next child repeats this and the activity continues in this way so that the 'tunnel' is moving from one end to the other. A set time can be allowed for this activity and the number of times each team member crawled through the tunnel added up to see which team crawled the most.

Allow for ample space.

ACTIVITY
VALUE

Physical fitness, strength in weight bearing and basic body movements (crawling).

Trio shuffle

ACTIVITY

The class is divided into groups of three who stand one behind the other in a line. The children in the line put their hands on the shoulders of the person in front of them, forming a chain. The teacher can then give various commands and the groups must move around the hall and remain in a chain. For example, the group must all walk on tip toes, squat down, move around hopping on one leg or walk backwards around the hall.

VARIATIONS

- The groups may be larger to create more exciting and challenging tasks.
- The children may create their own tasks or movement sequences.

ACTIVITY
VALUE

Co-operation, decision making in responding physically to a verbal command.

Over the legs relay

ACTIVITY

In pairs, the group sits down opposite their partners with their legs stretched out so that their feet are touching – all the pairs are in a line together like a railway track. Each couple is given a number. When the teacher calls out a number, that couple must run clockwise down inside and over the legs of the other pairs sitting on the floor, and then round the outside and, finally, back to their original place. This is repeated with other numbers being called out.

VARIATION

- Names or colours may be called out instead of numbers, and other tasks can be used instead of running, e.g. walking, skipping, jumping.

ACTIVITY VALUE

Eye–foot co-ordination, developing reaction time and anticipation.

Triads

The class is divided into groups of three. They go and stand inside three hoops which are laid out in a triangle shape with each hoop joined together by rope or string. The children hold the hoops up at waist height and take it in turns being the leader walking around the hall.

VARIATIONS

- The arrangement of the hoops can be changed to have a circle or square or even a chain of hoops attached together.
- Obstacles could be set up around the hall for the children to negotiate whilst travelling within the hoops.

EQUIPMENT

Hoops and string.

ACTIVITY VALUE

Offers some children a feeling of safety and security travelling in the hoops, and develops spatial awareness.

Blanket slide

ACTIVITY

The class is divided into groups of three or four. One child lies on a blanket with two or three other children holding the top corners. They slowly slide the child around the hall. They then take it in turns to lie on the blanket.

VARIATIONS

- An obstacle course could be set up around the hall comprising objects of different colours and textures.
- The blanket can be dragged in straight lines, zigzags, curves or circles, etc.
- If four children hold each corner of the blanket, then the child lying on it can be swayed or rocked from side to side in a swaying motion.

EQUIPMENT

One blanket per group.

ACTIVITY VALUE

Especially beneficial to children who have severe mobility difficulties and will enjoy the sensation of being swayed or dragged on the blanket.

Chariots

In groups of four with two mats per group, two children kneel down next to each other on all fours, making sure that their backs are as flat as table tops. A third child sits astride the two on all fours, with the fourth child supporting the rider by holding him or her at the waist. As a unit, the 'chariot' rocks back and forth slowly and then can venture to move forward (provided there are sufficient mats!) The teacher must ensure even distribution of size and weight wherever possible.

They then change positions.

ACTIVITY
VALUE

Co-operation, ability to take weight on a stable base (hands and knees) and to co-ordinate rhythmic movement as a unit.

Balloon volleyball

ACTIVITY

Small teams of four or five per side is recommended. Each team is positioned either side of the net. The object of the game is to keep the balloon in your opposing team's area by tapping the balloon over the net, and not allowing the balloon to touch the floor on your own team's side.

VARIATIONS

- If the game lacks fluency, bring in more balloons or lower the net so that hits can go over, or possibly shorten the court so that more players are involved.

- Simplify the rules, e.g. the first team to get three points; every team player must touch the balloon before it goes over the net; or, other parts of the body can be used to hit the balloon. Remember, success for every player is important.

EQUIPMENT

Badminton net and stands, balloons.

ACTIVITY VALUE

Co-operation, eye–hand co-ordination, spatial aware-ness, basics of striking skills.

Velcro fishing

The children sit in a circle. Each are given a unihoc stick to hold. At the bottom of the curved end of every stick is attached a small piece of velcro.

In the middle of the circle on the floor are a number of shuttlecocks spread out and standing upright. On the top bulbous end of each shuttlecock is placed the other half of velcro. By simply manoeuvering the unihoc stick over the shuttlecocks, the children attempt to fasten the shuttlecocks to the sticks, lift them up in the air and grab them like fish out of water.

VARIATIONS

- Using velcro in this way opens up endless possibilities of games and activities. Relay races are one alternative, where, one at a time, each team member runs with a stick to a shuttlecock in a hoop. This can continue until all team members have retrieved a shuttlecock from their hoops.

- For wheelchair users, velcro can be an independence promoter. In a game of badminton, for example, velcro can be stuck to both the shuttlecock and at the end of the racquet. In the course of a game, when the shuttle hits the floor, the person in the wheelchair can simply retrieve it for themselves by placing the end of their racquet on top of the shuttle, and continue to play.

EQUIPMENT Unihoc sticks, shuttlecocks, small tabs of velcro.

ACTIVITY VALUE Eye–hand co-ordination, concentration and promoting independence.

Pulling the basket

ACTIVITY

A rectangular PE basket or something similar has a long rope (3–4 m) attached at each end of it. Six or so children are lined up at each end of the rope behind a cone or marker and have one bean bag each.

The rope is pulled by the children at one end, thus bringing the basket towards them. Once it passes their marker, one child places his or her bean bag in the basket. Once this is done, the children at the other end pull the basket towards them and they repeat the process of placing a bean bag in the basket. This procedure of either pulling or slackening the rope depending on which end the basket is travelling to continues until all the children have put their bean bags in the basket. Two teams can compete to fill baskets full of bean bags using more ropes and more baskets.

EQUIPMENT

Two long ropes and PE baskets per group.

ACTIVITY VALUE

Co-operation and fine motor skills (gripping and pulling).

Slide time

ACTIVITY

Several benches are spread around the hall with mats placed across them to form slide humps. Each child is placed in a blanket with two adults straddling the bench and holding an end of the blanket each. The adults then slide the child in the blanket up and down the hump several times.

VARIATION

- Several bundles of equipment e.g. beanbags, quoits or ropes, can be laid out at various points near the benches so that each child can be placed upon them to feel their different textural qualities. They can be rocked from side to side in the blankets or simply laid down across the bundles.

- Each bundle of equipment can be wrapped in cling film to keep it together and to give it a more exciting and investigative appeal.

EQUIPMENT

Benches, mats, blankets, bundles of beanbags, quoits and ropes, cling film.

ACTIVITY VALUE

Experiencing sensation of sliding, rocking and exploration of various textures.

Skittle hit

ACTIVITY

The children sit in a circle on chairs, benches or wheelchairs. They each have a piece of guttering about 3 feet long. In the middle of the circle are placed several skittles. Each child is given some small balls that they roll down the guttering in an attempt to knock down the skittles.

Children who have difficulty in manipulating or gripping the ball down the guttering may need assistance in placing their hands or fingers on top of the ball. If they have enough mobility to lift up a few fingers to release the ball, they will be able to succeed in starting the ball rolling down the tubing.

VARIATION

This activity can be arranged individually as in Tenpin bowling, with the help of ramps or guttering to aid both the aim, release and speed of ball towards its target.

EQUIPMENT

Guttering, small balls, skittles, benches or chairs.

ACTIVITY
VALUE

Eye–hand co-ordination, aiming, judgement of release.

Skittle bombardment

ACTIVITY

A row of skittles is set out at each end of the hall and the children are divided into two teams. The centre section of the hall is designated a 'neutral zone'. Each team has to try and knock down their opponents skittles with volleyballs (or similar) whilst defending their own. Teams can only roll the ball along the ground, all throws take place from within teams' respective zone areas and no-one is allowed to enter the neutral zone. The winning team is the first to knock down all the opponent's skittles or to knock down most skittles in a given time.

```
Δ                                          Δ
Δ   X        NEUTRAL             O   Δ
Δ        X                    O      Δ
Δ   X        ZONE                O   Δ
Δ        X                    O      Δ
Δ   X                            O   Δ
Δ                                          Δ

    X ———————▶      ◀——————— O
```

EQUIPMENT   Skittles, balls and coloured bibs (two types).

ACTIVITY
VALUE   Basic ball skills (stopping, rolling, aiming) spatial awareness, and perceptual awareness.

Elastic skittle ball

Each child has an airflow ball (a plastic ball with holes in it) to which a length of elastic is tied. The other end of the elastic is taped down to the floor. The length of the elastic may vary according to the ability of the child.

The children can push or propel the balls away from themselves without having to move to retrieve them, as the elastic should bring the balls back!

After various free explorations with both pushing and throwing skills, more specific targets can be introduced. For example, skittles can be placed at a set distance away from the child, who attempts to knock them down by pushing or throwing the ball at them. Team games can also be introduced, such as the first team to knock down a certain amount of skittles.

VARIATION The balls can be attached to bats or small wooden racquets, rather than the floor, or hockey or unihoc sticks can be used to strike them from a stationary position.

Other pair or partner games can be devised in which the players take turns either to kick, strike or throw the ball in a variety of different ways.

EQUIPMENT Airflow balls of various sizes, elastic, masking tape, bats and unihoc sticks, skittles.

ACTIVITY VALUE Eye–hand co-ordination, more practice time, less retrieving time!

4 Large Group Activities

The large group activities contained in this section comprise mainly co-operative games which focus on participation. They present youngsters with opportunities to work with, explore, enjoy and have fun with others in an environment and context of co-operation. This will entail keeping the children *involved*, giving them a sense of *acceptance* and establishing an atmosphere of *enjoyment*.

Most of the activities offer variations so that, for children experiencing difficulty, appropriate modifications can be made, so that relative success is achievable. This responsibility lies in the teacher's observation in identifying needs and acting upon those needs.

Special equipment, such as parachutes and earthballs (very large beach balls) can be used in an exciting way to create large group games and promote social interaction through participation in a challenging way. Other games use little or no equipment and rely upon the collective physical arrangement of the group in creating its own physical dynamics.

I hope that the activities will also encourage and initiate further fresh movement game possibilities, but for this teachers will need to look beyond the activity to what kind of learning experiences are offered within it.

Car wash

ACTIVITY The class divides into two lines which face each other on hands and knees with a gap of two feet between them. One child from the end of line A crawls down the gap or tunnel like a car in a car wash, and all the children 'wash' gently by rubbing and stroking the car as it travels down the line. A child from the end of line B continues and alternately all the children travel through the car wash. When arriving at the end, each child rejoins his or her corresponding line and the process continues.

NB It might be wise to use a line of mats for the children to crawl down.

EQUIPMENT   Mats.

ACTIVITY   Social, co-operative and imaginative activity.

Bubble burst

ACTIVITY   In a circle, the children hold hands and they crouch down on their ankles. The whole group is to imagine that they are a large balloon that needs to be filled up with air until it pops. So while holding hands the children blow and slowly get taller and taller until they are all on tip toes. When the teacher says 'bang' they all flop down on to their ankles in a small curled shape. This can be repeated several times.

ACTIVITY
VALUE   Co-operation, balance, support and timing.

Circle rub

ACTIVITY   The children all stand in a circle facing the same way. They then all sit down with their legs astride, making sure they are cradling the person in front and being cradled themselves. The teacher calls out several tasks that each child has to perform on the back of the person in front. For example, massage their shoulder, finger chops on their backs, slide or rub fingers up and down their spine. Finally, they all lie down so that their heads are resting on the stomach of the person behind them!

ACTIVITY VALUE   Co-operation and an enjoyable way to end a session.

Keep bouncing

ACTIVITY   The children have a ball each (volleyball size) and are spread in a semi-circle around the teacher. The teacher gives various commands and to whatever is said the children must keep bouncing the balls as well as performing the command. For example, the teacher may say 'stand on one leg', 'sit down', 'kneel down' or 'jump with two feet', yet all the while the children must bounce their balls.

VARIATION
- Adapt the ball size to make it easier for some children.

EQUIPMENT   One ball per child.

ACTIVITY VALUE   Development of basic ball skill action (bouncing), using eye–hand co-ordination.

Circle pass

The group sits down in a large circle on the floor where five balls or more (depending on the size of the group) are distributed to children around the circle. On the word 'go' the children pass the balls clockwise from person to person as quickly as they can, as the object of the game is not to be caught with two balls at once. Start the game slowly so children can grasp the idea, and then gradually get faster.

VARIATIONS
- Give more balls out at the beginning of the game so that more people are active.
- The children could use their feet to pass the ball to each other, or other body parts.

EQUIPMENT
Sponge balls.

ACTIVITY VALUE
Eye–hand co-ordination, basics of grasping and releasing or giving and receiving.

Tell the time

ACTIVITY

A large clock-face with numbers but without the hands is marked on the floor. The children stand in a line from the twelve down to number six to indicate the time as half past twelve. The teacher then calls out a certain time, and the group have to organise themselves into two lines (long and short hands), from the central point out to the appropriate number. The teacher should help organise the first few called out, which should be fairly easy to begin with, e.g. 3 o'clock or 9.30, etc.

ACTIVITY
VALUE

Group co-operation, number recognition.

Getting in and out

ACTIVITY

The class form a circle and link arms tightly. Two children are asked to go in the middle and two children to go outside the circle. The children in the middle must try to get out of the circle and the two outside must try to get in. The circle of children must not let them in or out and must keep linked up tightly. Change the children outside and inside the circle fairly frequently.

ACTIVITY
VALUE

Co-operation, static strength.

Snakeskin

ACTIVITY

The group divides into teams of about ten. Each team stands in a line facing the same way. Each child bends over and, reaching between their legs with their right hand, grasps the left hand of the player behind. The child at the back of the line lies down and as he or she does so, the next player shuffles backwards, straddling the prostrate body and lies down behind, still holding hands. This continues until the whole group is lying down. The 'skin' can be put back on the snake by reversing the action until all the players are standing up.

ACTIVITY VALUE

Co-operation and support from team members.

Log roll

ACTIVITY

The group lie down on their stomachs in a line closely bunched up. The child at the end stands up and starts to crawl on hands and knees over the bodies until he or she gets to the end of the line. He or she lies down at the end of the line and the next child starts the pattern again. This is repeated until everyone has crawled over the line of bodies and, in so doing, moved the line from one end of the hall to the other.

NB This activity should be done in bare feet to avoid unnecessary discomfort!

ACTIVITY VALUE

Co-operation, trust.

Knots

ACTIVITY

Depending on how large the class is, the whole group forms a circle (ten children maximum). They slowly walk to the middle and grasp a pair of hands or arms opposite them. They then hold still and slowly, one at a time, try to unravel themselves by either climbing over or under arms, legs or bodies. This activity shouldn't last too long as the teacher may have considerable supervision to organise.

ACTIVITY VALUE

Co-operation and communication.

Pass and run

ACTIVITY

The children form a large circle. A large ball is passed by hand clockwise around the circle once. On the second time round, once a child has passed the ball, they must also run clockwise round the circle and get back to their place before the ball does, so that they are ready again to pass it and run! As this activity may become complex to learn, it is advised to go through it slowly before attempting it at speed.

VARIATION

• The group may have to be broken up into small groups, so that the concept of pass and run can be successfully grasped.

EQUIPMENT

One ball per group or circle.

ACTIVITY VALUE

Eye–hand co-ordination, physical fitness and timing.

Hands and feet

ACTIVITY

Hand and feet shapes are made from card and stuck down with blutack around the hall floor and walls. Much thought has to be given to the positioning of these shapes as the children will investigate them by matching hands onto cut-out hands and feet onto cut-out feet. Hands and feet can be stuck either close together, wide apart, on top of each other, criss crossing, diagonally apart etc. The teacher must ensure that the matching is easy and successful at first and then progresses with more challenging movements.

VARIATIONS

- A track or trail of hands and feet can be laid out for the children to follow.
- Obstacles can be added that the children have to negotiate whilst still following the path of feet and/or hands.

EQUIPMENT

Cut out hands and feet arranged as decided by the teacher.

ACTIVITY VALUE

Development of basic motor function (walking and tracking) and negotiating pathways.

Bubble plastic

ACTIVITY

A strip of bubble plastic (used for parcel wrapping insulation) is taped down across the hall floor. The children spread out along it and explore its exciting properties by jumping, crawling, slapping all different parts of their bodies on it. It will snap, crackle and pop all over the place!

EQUIPMENT

Large strip of bubble plastic.

ACTIVITY VALUE

The plastic will help to initiate movement and can be investigated for its textural qualities.

Sack slug walk

ACTIVITY

Each child has a dustbin liner that they sit in like a sleeping bag. They then travel around the hall by shuffling on their bottoms.

VARIATIONS

- The children can explore a variety of movement possibilities inside the dustbin bag. For example, lying down inside it and sliding around the hall, standing up and jumping, rolling backwards and forwards etc.

- If the bag is big enough, have two or three children inside one liner, to work co-operatively together in moving.

- The children could have obstacles to negotiate when moving around in the bags, e.g., through hoops, under sticks, or have various objects to collect while moving, for example, bean bags or small balls.

EQUIPMENT

One dustbin liner per child.

ACTIVITY
VALUE

Exploring and initiating movement possibilities, using basic body movements.

Chase the hoop

Each child has a hoop that he or she rolls and chases around the hall. The teacher then collects the hoops and the children line up at one end of the hall. The teacher calls out one of the children's names and at the same time rolls a hoop into the middle of the hall. The child whose name has been called runs to retrieve the hoop before it stops rolling. This continues until all the children have been called out.

VARIATIONS
- Two or three names can be called out at the same time.
- Children themselves can have turns rolling hoops for other children.

EQUIPMENT
Hoops.

ACTIVITY VALUE
Spatial and directional awareness, tracking and following a hoop, responding quickly to a command.

Ball passing game

ACTIVITY   The class is divided into number ones and number twos. All the number ones stand in hoops which are spread out on the hall floor. All the number twos have a ball each and on the command of the teacher, they have to pass the ball to as many number ones as they can. Number ones stand still in the hoops and when they receive a pass, they just simply pass it back. Number twos count how many passes they make. After a given time limit, they change over.

EQUIPMENT   Hoops and balls.

ACTIVITY VALUE   Basic passing technique, spatial awareness, catching and releasing, numeracy skills.

Grab the bean bag

ACTIVITY   The class get down on their hands and knees so that their backs are straight. The teacher places a bean bag on each back. They have to move slowly round the hall without dropping the bean bag.

VARIATIONS
- Place the bean bag on a different body part to make the activity either easier or more challenging for the child.
- Bring in an element of competition by saying that the children have to take or steal a bag from someone else's back, whilst guarding his or her own.

EQUIPMENT   One bean bag per child.

ACTIVITY VALUE   Basic body movement (crawling), spatial and peripheral awareness.

Zone games

ACTIVITY

Teams are set up as in the diagram, with benches or cones separating the zones areas. Teams are designated alternate zones with a prescribed amount of players in each zone. Players are free to move only in their allocated zones, trying to get the ball to their team colleagues nearest to the goal or baskets.

Figure 2

The setting up of 'zones' gives youngsters lacking in co-ordination or confidence time to catch the ball, turn, dribble and pass without any confrontation from opposition.

Once the teacher perceives that the children are becoming successful and competent at these skills, the benches can slowly be taken away and zones can begin to merge until no benches are used and a full game is operational. This type of conditioned zone game can be used not only in basketball or netball, but also in hockey and football, using cones instead of benches to outline the zone areas.

EQUIPMENT

Balls, benches or cones.

ACTIVITY VALUE

Non-threatening way to grasp basic principles of team games and successful way of learning basic skills within a conditioned game situation.

Hoop ball

ACTIVITY

This is a conditioned game which can be used in football or hockey. A five-or six-a-side game is set up, with two hoops placed wide at the wings on the left and right sides in the centre area. One person from each team stands inside either hoop A or B. The idea is that each team, before they can have an attempt at goal, must pass the ball to their respective team member inside the hoop. In this way children learn to pass the ball wide and use space.

VARIATION

• Use four hoops (two on each side) with two people from each team nominated to stand inside. This time, before an attempt at goal can be made, the ball must be passed to both 'hoop' people, thus switching the play from wing to wing.

EQUIPMENT

Hoops.

ACTIVITY
VALUE

Makes children aware of creating and using space efficiently and spreading play around the whole playing area.

Archball rounders

ACTIVITY

The area of play is marked by two parallel lines 10 metres apart. The class is divided into a batting team and a fielding team. The players in the batting team line up one behind the other on the near line, with all of the fielders positioned behind the end line.

The first batting player starts on the near line and throws or kicks (depending on ability) a ball into the playing area, then attempts to move around his or her own team as many times as possible until told to stop by the fielding team.

Once the batting player has hit the ball into the playing area, the whole fielding team runs to try and retrieve it. The rest of the team form a line behind whoever picks it up and the ball is passed overhead down towards the last back player who then calls 'stop' and the batter stops running. After the batters have all had a turn, and their runs totalled up, the teams change over.

VARIATIONS

- Depending upon ability, the teacher can act as bowler, thus controlling both teams and awarding extra runs for good fielding and batting.

- Balls of different sizes and textures can be used to give success to batters, e.g. large sponge balls.

- Some batters will find it easier to hit, throw or kick a stationary ball. Teachers' observation in gauging individual needs will be crucial.

EQUIPMENT

Variety of different balls, chalk to mark out lines.

ACTIVITY VALUE

Basic striking skills, basic retrieving skills, eye–hand co-ordination, physical fitness development.

Skittle ball

The game is played by two teams and the aim is to knock down the opponent's skittle which is placed on a mat or hoop and situated at opposing ends of the playing area. There is no running allowed with the ball, no physical contact and no attacker or defender allowed within the circle or on a mat where the skittle is. Rules can be adapted to serve the needs of the children playing. Scoring can be over a set time limit or the first to a set number of skittle knock downs.

VARIATIONS

- This activity can be played kneeling or sitting down.
- Use more skittles for both teams to knock down to make it easier and more exciting.
- Shorten the playing area and number of players.

EQUIPMENT

Skittles, mats or hoops, ball.

ACTIVITY VALUE

Principles of attack and defending a target, basic passing and aiming skills and co-operatively working within a team game environment.

Bucket ball

There are two teams, one batting and one fielding.

They line up facing each other about 10 metres apart. The batting team all have a ball and on the word 'go' from the teacher, have to throw them anywhere in the playing area. Once thrown, the first person in the batting team has to run round the whole batting team as many times as possible until the fielders shout 'stop'.

The fielders simply have to retrieve all the balls thrown and place them in a bucket situated in the middle between the two teams. When all balls are safely deposited in the bucket they shout 'stop' and the runner stops running, counts the number of runs made, and the process begins again. This continues until all the batting team have run, when all runs are totalled up, and the teams change over. The team with the most runs wins.

VARIATIONS
- The balls can be kicked instead of thrown from the batting team.
- The teacher can add or deduct runs for good and bad fielding or batting.

EQUIPMENT
Large bucket or bin, balls of various sizes.

ACTIVITY VALUE
Spatial awareness, throwing and retrieving skills, physical fitness and co-operation.

Cross over

ACTIVITY The children stand evenly around the parachute and they are all given a number. They bend their knees slightly and grip the 'chute, holding it at waist height in two hands. On the command 'mushroom' all the children stand up and raise their arms straight up in the air, so that the 'chute makes a mushroom shape.

While it is up in the air the teacher calls out two numbers. The children with these numbers must simply make their way across the circle before the 'chute deflates. This is repeated with two different numbers.

VARIATION
- As the 'chute goes up, the teacher could call out, for example, a colour that some children are wearing and those children must travel across the circle before the 'chute comes down.

EQUIPMENT Parachute.

ACTIVITY Co-operation and upper body strength.
VALUE

102

Cat and mouse

ACTIVITY

The group is spaced evenly round a parachute. Three or so children are chosen to be mice and they go beneath the 'chute. Three children are chosen to be cats and they go on top of the 'chute and crawl on their hands and knees around it. The remainder of the group billow the parachute so that the 'mice' beneath cannot be seen. The cats try to catch the mice by touching them.

Teachers note that, as this game can be wearing on the arms, cats and mice should be changed frequently so that everyone has a turn and a rest from waving the 'chute for too long!

EQUIPMENT

Parachute.

ACTIVITY
VALUE

Co-operation, spatial awareness and large muscle movements (upper body).

Inside a tent

ACTIVITY

The children are spread evenly around a parachute. After a count of three, they lift up the parachute, keeping their arms straight up in the air. However, instead of leaving their arms up in the air, the children bring the parachute over their heads, behind their backs and sit down on it. This will have the effect that everyone is inside a tent. A ball can be at hand, which can be passed inside the tent, across from child to child.

NB Some children may find being inside the parachute uncomfortable, so be aware not to leave them underneath for too long.

EQUIPMENT

Parachute.

ACTIVITY
VALUE

Co-operation and social awareness.

Rollerball

ACTIVITY

The group divides into two teams, which stand in two circles, one circle inside the other with children facing each other and with enough space between them for an earthball (or very large beach ball) to roll around on the ground. One player stands in the space between the circles on the opposite side of the circle to the ball. This player has to catch the ball by running forwards round the circle. The rest of the group keep the ball rolling round the circle as fast as possible to avoid it being caught.

EQUIPMENT

Earthball or large beach ball.

ACTIVITY
VALUE

Co-operation and eye–hand co-ordination.

106

Earthball kick and push

ACTIVITY

The children form a large circle and kneel down. The teacher throws an earthball (or a very large beach ball) into the middle and the children have to push it across the circle to each other using only their hands.

VARIATIONS

- If the children sit down, the soles of the feet can be used to kick-push the ball across.
- A child can stand in the middle of the circle and try to avoid being touched by the ball while it is being pushed or kicked across the circle.
- Widen or reduce the size of the circle accordingly so that the children can participate easily.

EQUIPMENT

One earthball or large beach ball.

ACTIVITY VALUE

Co-operation, eye–hand/foot co-ordination.

Useful reading

B.A.A.L.P.E. (1989) *Physical Education for Children with Special Educational Needs in Mainstream Education.* Leeds: White Line Press.

Barlin, A. and Kalev, N. (1989) *Hello Toes! Movement Games for Children.* Princeton: Princeton Book Company.

Booth, D. (1968) *Games for Everyone.* Canada: Pembroke Publishers.

Brown, A. (1987) *Active Games for Children with Movement Problems.* London: Harper and Row.

Heseltine, P. (1987) *Games for All Children.* Oxford: Basil Blackwell.

Loscher, A. (1990) *Everybody Play!.* Toronto: Sports Book Publishers.

Masheder, M. (1989) *Let's Play Together.* London: Green Print.

Orlick, T. (1978) *The Cooperative Sports and Games Book.* New York: Pantheon Books.

Price, R. (1980) *Physical Education and the Physically Handicapped Child.* London: Lepus Books.

Russell, J. (1988) *Graded Activities for Children with Motor Difficulties.* Cambridge: Cambridge University Press.

Stewart, D. (1990) *The Right to Movement: Motor Development in Every School.* London: Calmer Press.

Sherborne, V. (1990) *Developmental Movement for Children.* Cambridge: Cambridge University Press.

Watson, B. (1984) *Physical Education for Poorly Co-ordinated Children.* Australia: Achper Publications.

Wetton, P. (1988) *Physical Education in the Nursery and Infant School.* London: Croom Helm.

Activities Index